EXPRESSIONS FROM THE HEART

Frenchel R. Martin

EXPRESSIONS FROM THE HEART
Copyright © 2007 Frenchel R. Martin

All Rights Reserved

ISBN: 978-1-59352-288-9

Published by:
Christian Services Network
833 Broadway, Suite #201
El Cajon, CA 92021
Toll Free: 1-866-484-6184
www.CSNbooks.com

No part of this publication may be reproduced, stored in a retrieval system, or transmitted in any way by any means – electronic, mechanical, photocopy, recording, or otherwise, without the prior permission of the copyright holder, except as provided by USA copyright law.

Cover picture photographed by Oscar L. Martin, Jr.

Printed in the United States of America.

DEDICATION

IN MEMORY OF

My loved ones gone before: My parents, Clyde and Octavia Patterson, and my siblings Virgil, Lindsey, Jennie, Clyde, and James.

DEDICATED TO

My existing and future grandchildren and great-grandchildren: DeNae, Mariah, Remi, Quentin, Kendall, and Amya, who although not the children of my womb, they are the children of my heart.

My sons Oscar Jr. and Kenji, the ones I love with a love that is beyond measure, and my daughter-in-law Charmaine who is treasured and very dear to my heart.

My husband, Oscar, the love of my life, my soul mate, and my best friend.

With all my love,
frm

Trust in the Lord with all your heart and lean not on your own understanding. In all your ways acknowledge him and he will make your path straight.
(Proverbs 3:5-6)

Thanks

Although the idea of compiling the contents of this booklet has been a distant thought for many years, I was somewhat reluctant to move forward because of the nagging fear that my "heart expressions" were not artistic enough to share with others than for whom written. However, as I became more centered in Christ, and more at ease with this talent, I embarked on acknowledging, embracing and giving thanks for the flair to create a word picture of my thoughts.

Thanks and appreciation to my husband, children, family, and friends for their ongoing encouragement and support in completing this project. I am also grateful for their confidence that my thoughts were something to be shared. To those individuals who invited me to create, edit, and critique articles, and as a consequence elevated and enhanced my confidence and skills, thank you for your trust in my judgment and that I had something meaningful to contribute.

My desire is that, in some diminutive way, the words on these pages will lift your spirit and bring joy to your soul.

Table of Contents

Dedication iii
Thanks v

Chapter One 9
   Celebrating Birthdays
Chapter Two 39
   Celebrating Marriage
Chapter Three 43
   Honoring Mothers
Chapter Four 51
   Honoring Fathers
Chapter Five 55
   Thanks
Chapter Six 61
   Holiday Celebrations
Chapter Seven 67
   Graduation Celebrations
Chapter Eight 69
   An Assortment of Poems
Chapter Nine 81
   Tributes
Chapter Ten 91
   Praises of Jubilare

CHAPTER ELEVEN 95
   Sympathy
CHAPTER TWELVE 97
   Remembering Birthdays
CHAPTER THIRTEEN 103
   Magnificent – Marriage Moments
CHAPTER FOURTEEN 105
   Congratulations
CHAPTER FIFTEEN 109
   Meaningful Sharings
CHAPTER SIXTEEN 111
   Soothing Your Sorrows
CHAPTER SEVENTEEN 115
   Christmas
CHAPTER EIGHTEEN 119
   Additional Poems
ORDER PAGE 125

Chapter One

Celebrating Birthdays

Another birthday and oh what a great blessing,
To know who you are and not have to be guessing. Although there are everyday burdens that we all must bear,
If you trust in the Savior there will be no need for despair.
You should trust in a God who loves you this way,
The One who blesses you day after day.
So enjoy this day and all the blessings it brings
And continue to give thanks to our risen King.

We wish you a fantastic birthday celebration. God has blessed you with nineteen years of grace, so remember to give thanks for His goodness. Always remember, we love you today more than yesterday, and you wouldn't believe how much we loved you yesterday.

As we travel the highway of life, we encounter individuals who are truly blessed by being the recipients of a wealth of wisdom and knowledge.
You are blessed with both,
enhanced by character traits of a vivacious personality, generous heart, and a compassionate spirit.
We wish you contentment and continued faith
in the Lord as you continue life's journey.

We hope your eighty-first birthday celebration
is really, really great,
And that you, family, and friends have
a wonderful date.
Remember, birthdays are special and gifts from God,
So glory in His blessings and give praises
to our Father above.

Today is your twentieth birthday,
We think that's a blessing and super great;
We're anticipating changes and praying
A new direction you will instigate.
You have talent and such a good heart,
All you have to do is make a prudent restart.
Your parents, grandparents, family, and friends
Are always eager to support you
and offer a helping hand.
We encourage you to embrace biblical
doctrine and take a positive stance.

Chapter One: Celebrating Birthdays

God has blessed you and keeps
giving you chance after chance,
And a family that loves you and
wants you to advance.
So take this loving counsel to heart,
Analyze your life and begin today to make a fresh start.

He was born in Oklahoma and reared in Merced,
But that special gift from Texas is what stays in his head,
As that's where he met his wife and years later they wed.
She is the delight of his heart, and she gave him three children
Who are God-fearing, attractive, obedient, and smart.
They planned this birthday surprise to demonstrate their love,
So allow them some slack
And don't give them any yakety-yak.
Celebrating with family and friends is always a good thing;
So enjoy this special day and all that it brings,
Remembering to give thanks to God, who is in control of all things.

I acknowledge that this special birthday card is somewhat late,
But that's doesn't negate the fact that we are going to celebrate.

So select a delightful place and tell us where to meet
So we can chat, enjoy each other's company and have something scrumptious to eat.
Pick up the phone, make that call and let us know,
Because we, your friends, are excited and ready to go.

You have been blessed with another great year,
To honor, praise, and share His good deeds,
As He is always there, whatever your needs.
You must remember to thank Him for his unfailing grace,
For where would you be without His mercy and Him giving you faith.
So enjoy this day and all that it brings
As you continue to obey and praise His holy name.

Birthday wishes from friend one and friend two,
We look forward to Sunday fellowship
in adjacent church pews.
We're Sunday morning neighbors,
and that is really great,
United in Christ, and that's something
we should all celebrate.
You are honored to be another year older
and that's really a blessing,
We've often pondered your age,
but we'll just have to keep guessing.
Celebrate and enjoy this special day with family

Chapter One: Celebrating Birthdays

and friends,
Giving thanks that His Word is instilled within.
Give praise for blessings this year will bring,
Remembering always to honor and praise
His holy Name.

Child of my womb and love of our hearts,
We are blessed to have been chosen to give you a start.
Wonderful son and brother of one,
We are incredibly proud and truly love you.
So many blessings you have been given,
And so many years of virtually carefree living.
Reflect on His goodness and all that it brings
And give thanks to Him, the One that reigns.

It's another birthday celebration
with unnumbered blessings,
Being thankful and learning from day-to-day lessons.
Loved ones and friends you continue to share,
With a few earthly burdens that we all must bear.
Keep trusting in the Savior,
and there will be no need for despair;
Just enjoy new mercies each day
from a God who is always there.
You must trust in a God who loves us this way
And keeps blessing you day after day.
So enjoy this day and all that it brings
And continue to give thanks to our risen King.

Sisters are wonderful blessings from above,
albeit we sometimes disagree,
But forever we love and allow each to be free.
Birthdays are special,
so we are thankful and cherish each year
By being appreciative of cards,
gifts, and birthday wishes that are music to our ears.
You are my sister and I am thankful for the bond,
I treasure our friendship,
shared birth month, and beyond.
Reflect on this birthday and all that it brings.
Be thankful for good health, loved ones,
and blessings each day brings,
And give praise,
as someday you will reside in His domain.

Birthdays are delightful, especially for a sister like you,
So we're sending this card to wish you love from us two.
We wish you joy and happiness on your special day
And many more years of celebrating this jubilant way.
We offer up prayers for your good health to behold,
But most of all that God is the keeper of your soul.
So give thanks for His goodness and all that it brings
And never forget that He's in control of all things.

You are a very special niece in so many ways;
We wish you lots of happiness in future days.
We love you and respect the choices you've made.

Chapter One: Celebrating Birthdays

We treasure your kinship, shared joys, visits of bygone days.
We pray for your guidance and success in all that you do.
You are such a great person, and you can make it through,
So we are praying that all your positive aspirations and dreams come true.

Celebrating
   Spirit of our faith in Christ and Christian fellowship
   Integrity and loyalty of our sister-sister love
   Strength and value of our family sisterhood
   Trust and love of our sister-sister bond
   Encirclement and esteem of our family unity
   Respectfulness of trivial differences; appreciative of loved shared experiences
   Souls connected by lineage, but loved by choice.

Celebrating your birthday for:
   Generosity shown during adolescence
   Love of family unity
   Organizational abilities which I strive to emulate
   Resourcefulness and your take charge stance
   Innovative cleverness during adversity
   Always being there for us
My prayer is that God is the keeper of your soul.

It's your birthday, and I think you are:
    Marvelous in your sensitivity toward others
    Available consistently to family members
    Respectful, kind, and a gracious sister
    Youthful in your outlook and approach to life with zest and zeal.

Birthday's are gifts from God, so:
    Look over your life and decide what is appropriate for you to do.
    Institute these changes and all of us will be available to assist you.
    Never doubt that we care and love you much.
    Decide to live your life the way you want, but be mindful of keeping in touch.
    Remember the pleasurable times and all the love that we share.
    Ingrain in your heart that you are special and we all care.
    Always rejoice in the blessings given and commit your life to Christian living.

Chapter One: Celebrating Birthdays

L is for your love and longing exhibited for God and family.
A is for your affable and amicable personality when intermingling with others.
V is for your vivacious and vibrant pursuit in understanding God's Word.
E is for your energetic and enthusiastic approach to life's challenges.
R is for your reliability and resoluteness in committing to biblical doctrine.
N is for your nurturing style and striving for nobility.

L is for your unquenchable love for Christ and His precepts.
E is for your enthusiasm, exhilaration, and endurance to live by faith.
O is for your obedience and overwhelming desire for a Christ-centered life.
N is for your novice approach in hearing and sharing the Word.

Celebrate another year of expanded maturity and embrace the coming year.
Hold dear and cherish loved ones that enhance your joy.
Appreciate life's valleys as they are essential to mountain experiences.
Rejoice in the splendor and daily abundance of God's blessings.

M is for being such a magnificent daughter and the joy you bring to loved ones.
A is for your agreeable personality and the smile on your beautiful face.
R is for remembering to be kind and thoughtful to your family and friends.
I is for inspiration demonstrated to others and facing new challenges.
A is for assisting Mom, being a terrific big sister, and teaching her words and games.
H is for the happiness you bring to the lives of those around you.

Happy Thirteenth Birthday! We are:
Delighted God sent you to be a member of our family.
Excited each time you call, write, or come to spend time with us.
Nostalgic when you are away from us.
Adamant about remembering you in our prayers.
Enthusiastic as we observe you change from an adorable infant into a beautiful teenager.

We love you because of who you are:
Marvelous
Ambitious
Resourceful
Innovative
Articulate
Helpful
We wish you a fun-loving eleventh-year birthday celebration!

Chapter One: Celebrating Birthdays

We love you because you are:
Really a pretty little girl, nice daughter, sister, and granddaughter.
You are
Easy to love, obedient to your parents, nice to your sister and school friends.
You always
Make us laugh, lift our spirits, draw us pictures, and make us happy when you visit
You are very
Interesting to talk with, and we hope you have a wonderful birthday.

A birthday is one of God's many blessings!
Honoring God's principles for eternal life
Embracing the fruit of the Spirit in daily lifestyle choices
Loving your neighbor as yourself
Enjoying fellowship with other believers
Never forgetting to give thanks for the joy others bring.

You have been blessed to reach six scores,
Surrounded by many loved ones and so much more.
But always remember, your birthday is special and a gift from the Lord,
Therefore be ever so thankful, and blessings do not hoard.

We pray that you have the benefit of daily peace and are inspired by God's mercies, blessings, and His saving grace. Use this day forward to demonstrate thankfulness for His enduring compassion.

Although one could say your "special day" is just like any other day, but one could also consider it as God's gift of a once-a-year day to celebrate the person He created you to be. You could take this opportunity to pause and ponder where you are in the process of becoming that person. You could also use this "special day" as a prayer-filled day and give "thanks" for past blessings, now blessings, and look forward and thank Him for honoring "please" in the future blessings.

Celebrating, because you are:
    Bold in embracing biblical doctrine and sharing Christian values as guidelines for your life.
    Optimistic in facing day-to-day challenges in a world deficient in ethical principles and swarming with unrest.
    Beautiful and gentle in spirit, and your countenance is persuasive as you encounter the joys, trials, and tribulations of life.
    Brave in your stance of emotional and financial support to others, especially our aging and youth population.
    Innovative in your approach to sharing life experiences to ease the anguish of others and offer avenues to grasp a dilemma and reach a moral resolution.
    Enthusiastic in the manner our friendship developed into one of respect, trust, and Christian sisterhood.

Chapter One: Celebrating Birthdays

Birthdays are really special, and so are you;
We love you and think you are great, and also sort of cute.
So enjoy your birthday with family and friends
And look forward with anticipation as next year you will be ten.

Today our granddaughter is nine, but that's definitely not all;
She's beautiful, smart, and stands over four feet tall.
She is a daughter, big sister and a granddaughter that's super great.
She has a fantastic personality, the potential it takes
To aspire to great heights, and ambitions to bring her many delights.
She's kind, considerate, and brings great joy;
she shares all of her love and most of her toys.
To know her is to love her and that's not all,
As she influences the heart that encompasses it all.
We're happy and blessed that we are one family,
As you are greatly loved, and we cherish the unity.

I woke up this morning with a rather nagging thought,
Remembered today is your birthday; a card we must send without a doubt.
After a quick nap, I put on my thinking cap
And this is what I mapped out.
We worship together and sometimes share

Sunday dinners which are spirited and quite nice.
But what's really awesome is that we are
United in our faith and trust and belief in Jesus Christ.
You are truly a blessing and a gift from God,
And we send birthday greetings from the center of our hearts.
This is your special day, so celebrate this occasion with thanksgiving
As you are blessed to be counted amongst the living.

The angels awakened you this morning and for that you are truly blessed;
You were clothed in your right mind, knew who you were, and didn't have to guess.
Today is a new day that the Lord has made,
So celebrate and rejoice and give Him praise.
Reflect on bygone years and God's unwavering mercy and grace,
Give Him honor and biblical teachings strive to always embrace.
Accept this birthday wish and our modest token of love;
Always remember you are blessed as you belong to the Father above.

Quentin, today's your first birthday and we think that's really great,
But the fact that you are our great-grandson is really something we are delighted to celebrate.

Chapter One: Celebrating Birthdays

Many nights you've kept Mommy and Daddy and Grandmother awake;
But they must remember in raising kids that's included in the love of give and take.
We think you're terrific and just as handsome as a great-grandson can be;
We love you so much and pray always for your safety.
So obey Mom and Dad and don't put them through too many tests,
Because in loving and raising you they are to do their very best.
You are much too young to realize what life is all about,
But if you are obedient life will be less painful,
And you will be happy and grow up to be a delight.

You awakened this morning enjoying another of God's blessings,
You knew who you were and didn't have to be guessing.
You had use of your extremities and were clothed in your right mind,
The angels were obedient and aroused you on time.
God in His unwavering mercy is compassionate and gracious to you;
Your kindheartedness allows His generosity to flow to others through you.
Enjoy this birthday wish from friend one and friend two,
We are happy to have cultivated a friendship with the two of you.
We value your thoughtfulness and all that you so unselfishly do.

Eight is behind you and you have moved on to nine
We hope your birthday celebration was fun and you had a really great time
We are sorry this birthday card is a little late
We love you a lot and hope you saved us some ice cream and cake.

We send birthday greetings to our "brother in Christ" who we think is truly great,
Although thoughts of aging can sometime be somewhat daunting and difficult to take.
Remember our Lord has been generous, and you are wonderfully blessed,
So just keep celebrating the years as they are some of the best.
Embrace the added year and the favors it brings;
Always give honor and thanks to Christ the King.
Today is your birthday and that's really great,
We hope to be invited for dinner, ice cream, and cake.

It's wonderful to have been born and live in a country that's free,
But it's really a great blessing to be celebrating year ninety-three.
Give thanks each night as the day draws to an end;
Being ever so grateful that Jesus Christ lives within.
Give thanks each night on bended knees

Chapter One: Celebrating Birthdays

Because of His sacrifice you are spiritually free.
Give thanks always for His mercy and unwavering grace,
The hunger and endurance to run this Christian race.
Be thankful for waking each morning clothed in your right mind,
With thoughts of Jesus as He is merciful and ever so kind.

As we celebrate another year of gracefully aging, let us remember to give thanks for the blessings of family, friends, enjoyable health, and a host of everyday blessings that we oftentimes take for granted. I hope that this special day is spent reflecting on all the positive things in life, and that you are looking forward with a spirit of happiness and all the joy of experiencing the pleasures that are yet to come.

Today is your birthday, so how do you do?
When we awakened this morning, our thoughts were of you.
We gave thanks for our many blessings and, of course, we included you.
When reminiscing over my life on your birth of forty-plus years,
My heart rejoiced and my eyes overflowed with tears.

Our love has progressively matured over the years
As we continue to bond closer through valleys and hills.
We like you and love you for the things that you do,
And wouldn't consider trading you if there was a family coup.
We love you for this and we love you for that,
But a few of the reasons we love you include some of these facts:
You are our son.
You are the father of our grandchildren.
You are caring.
You are dependable.
You are loveable.
You are thoughtful.
You are trustworthy.
You are ours.

We are sending birthday wishes from friend one and friend two,
We are delighted to have formed a fantastic friendship with you.
Enjoy your day and all the blessings it brings
And continue to give thanks to the risen King.

You are a native of West Virginia, so elegant and fashionably tall,
A wonderful sister, mother and friend, but that's not all.
You are thoughtful, ingenious, dedicated, all rolled into

a beautiful ball,
And available to your family and friends whenever they call.
So pick up the phone and let's make a date,
We will all get together, eat, drink, and celebrate.

I awakened this morning with a somewhat nagging thought spinning about:
What should we give our son for his birthday that's great without a doubt?
You are another year older and truly blessed,
Including an attractive wife and beautiful daughters that are amongst the best.
There is no way of exceeding what you already have,
So here's a little something for a round of golf with your pals.

Today is your birthday and oh what a blessing;
God's angel woke you on time and not only that,
You were clothed in your right mind.
He is such an awesome God and you are His child;
He blessed you with another birthday, making family and friends smile.
You have so much to give thanks for, so much to give praise,
Continue to honor and obey, and in your life He will reign.

You wedded my sister, gosh what a great treat;
We're related by marriage and that's really nice.
But what's really awesome is that we are united
In our faith and belief in the Lord Jesus Christ.
We've enjoyed numerous vacations, some joyful and some with a little spice;
We also share adjacent church pews and Sunday dinners monthly once or twice.
We send birthday greetings to a "brother" who's really great,
Although thoughts of aging can sometimes be difficult to take.
Remember, our Lord has been merciful and you are superbly blessed,
So just keep celebrating the years as they are some of the best.
Embrace this added year and all that it brings,
Giving thanks to Christ the King as His reign is supreme.

He awakened you this morning to a beautiful new day,
Clothed in your right mind and preparing to get on your way.
Being Sunday morning classmates and enjoying our friendship is really great,
But, being united in Christ, now that's something to rejoice and celebrate.
We celebrate you being another year gifted, which is a wonderful blessing,

Chapter One: Celebrating Birthdays

And your continued obedience to His Word leads to inspiring lessons.
Celebrate and enjoy this special day with loved ones, family and friends,
Give thanks that His Word is true and instilled deep within.
Give praise for the blessings you can be assured this year will bring,
And remember always to honor and praise His holy name.

Nieces are very special people
And we really think you're super great,
So we are sending our birthday wishes to our niece
Who is quite smart and just turned eight.
It's now time to celebrate, so let's get together
And enjoy big portions of ice cream and cake.

Daughters-in-law are super special, and we think you are, too;
We send birthday wishes from hearts filled with love and truth.
This is your special day, so enjoy it with thanksgiving;
Give thanks for your blessings and that you're counted amongst the living.
You are such a great wife and a wonderful mother to boot;

We are delighted and proud that you are part of our troupe.

We are celebrating your twelfth birthday, and we thing that's great.
I hope your mom is serving more than just ice cream and store-bought cake.
Now that you are twelve and on your way to being a teen,
There are some things you should remember to keep your mind keen:
Make choices that will result in your family being proud,
Which includes limiting negative behavior and seldom talking loud.
Allow no one to devalue your talents and God-given worth,
As you were made and loved by Him who put you on this earth.
Listen to those who love you and have your best interest at heart,
As they will be there for encouragement and to give you a positive start.
Embrace biblical teachings, sing praises to Jesus Christ,
You will be rewarded and enjoy a joyful and blessed life.
Enjoy this birthday and all that it brings,
We think you are cute, have a beautiful smile and deserve great things.
So celebrate this birthday with family and friends,

Chapter One: Celebrating Birthdays

Remember, today is your special day, but just like Cinderella,
At midnight all this special treatment comes to an end.

Celebrate and enjoy your special day,
Realizing that each year is another blessing from God,
And you have a responsibility to make
The best of what's been given to you.

You were born and reared in West Virginia
And you stand approximately five feet eight inches tall;
You're strong in character and possess skills both large and small.
You have a delightful disposition that's appreciated and recognized by all;
A gentle spirit and respected for not being easily galled.
We take pleasure in having you as a sister and sister-in-law,
But not only that, you are a friend
And we think you're really super and wouldn't trade you as kin
For the California lottery win.

She trusts in a God that's full of love, mercy and grace,
And she lives life to reflect His glory
As one day she will see Him face-to-face.

She's married to her teen sweetheart, and that's really an awesome treat,
As not only does he admire her, he loves her from her head to her feet.
She is the apple of his eye and, without a doubt,
The choice of topping on his pie.
Her daughters and grandchildren love and respect her
And realize they are blessed to have her in their lives,
A person who is God fearing and incredibly wise.

We take pleasure in having met you, establishing a rapport and having you as our friend.
We think you're super and wouldn't trade your friendship for the California lottery win.
Enjoy your special day and all that it brings,
And give thanks to our Lord, the King of all kings.

You are our nephew and we couldn't be more proud;
Not only do we like you, but our love for you abounds.
You are charismatic, handsome, intelligent to boot,
And when we become dissolute, we know who to call for a little loot.
We send lots of cheers and birthday wishes from your favorite two.

Chapter One: Celebrating Birthdays

Remember birthday years are gifts from God, so give thanks, celebrate and enjoy.
Thank Him for years of happiness, family, friends, and all good deeds
As He is never slow in providing for all your needs.
All you have to do is trust Him and stay on bended knees.

Today is your birthday and we think that's just great;
We are anticipating and like the positive changes you have decided to make,
And praying for a new direction you will instigate.
We know you have many talents and such a good heart;
Now all you have to do is be committed to your optimistic restart.
Your family is always willing to give you a helping hand,
But first you must stand firm and keep performing, as we know you can.
God has blessed you and keeps giving you chance after chance,
And a family that really loves you and wants you to advance.

Sometimes we call you Jim and other times James,
But no matter what you're called, we are friends just the same.
You hail from Texas and stand over six feet tall;

Your wife encourages you to toe the line and that's not all,
As you try to be available whenever friends call.
Call us with a time and date,
So we can make plans to celebrate.

We are friends of your son and daughter-in-law and did not want to miss the opportunity to wish you happy birthday on this historic occasion. It is always a pleasure to say, "Many happy returns of the day," to a person who is the recipient of one hundred years of God's grace, mercy, and one who so boldly acknowledges Christ as the head of his life. We wish you contentment as you enjoy family and friends as they gather to pay homage to you as a son, brother, husband, father, grandfather, great-grandfather, and friend. We pray that God continues to bless and keep you in His care. Please accept our congratulations and best wishes.

Three score and more you have been blessed
And each morning His angels aroused you from a night of protection and bodily rest.
New mercies each morning day after day,
You can rejoice that you serve an all-powerful God who treats you this way.
It's such a blessing to believe and trust in a God who imparted His Word for us to obey.
Family and friends all love and respect you a lot;

Chapter One: Celebrating Birthdays

We are delighted to be included in your "friendship pot".
Frequent phone chats, although home visits are few,
But we have the assurance you are a friend through and through.
Enjoy these birthday wishes from friend one and friend two,
Our lives are enriched since becoming acquainted with you.
We present this bouquet of flowers with a soothing scent to breathe in,
Accompanied by an inspirational book to enjoy and share with loved ones and friends.
Rejoice in this birthday as you are His child, with no need to fret,
Because when you obey, He will be your safety net.

Share this birthday with loved ones, family and friends,
As they love you and want to help you celebrate over and over again.
We could say you look first-class for the age that you are,
But then we must remember who brought you this far.
We hope your birthday celebration was really great,
And now we expect to share in the enjoyment of eating homemade ice cream and delicious pound cake.

He woke you this morning and it was at the appropriate time,
And not only that, you were energetic and clothed in your right mind.
Today is your birth date, so family and friends came to celebrate
As we rejoice and observe your sixty-eighth birth date.
Remember to always honor and praise Him every day,
As our God is awesome and keeps blessing you in His own special way.
So enjoy this day, the joy and happiness it will undoubtedly bring,
And thank Him for past, present, and all future things.

Three score and more you have been given,
You show your thanks by your Christian living.
Three score and more you have been blessed,
Each morning the angels awaken you from a night of safety and bodily rest.
Three score and more you have been honored,
With many carefree years, unmerited bliss and few things to ponder.
God in His mercy and grace has been good to you;
Give Him thanks in all that He allows you to do
With a heart that allows blessings to flow to others through you.
God allows His angel to awaken you each morning with a soft gentle touch,
You should show thanks by praising and honoring Him much.

Chapter One: Celebrating Birthdays

God keeps blessing you day after day;
You should rejoice in the reality of serving
A God that's omnipotent, omnipresent, omniscient, and loves you in such a special way.
Celebrate this birthday with wonder and delight
As the stars in the sky, moon and the sun,
Give us assurance of a heavenly Father and Son.

Two score plus ten, you have been so beautifully blessed,
Your loved ones and friends came to help you celebrate and wish you the best.
Fifty is awesome, and to that we both can boldly attest.
Be mindful of not rushing forward, just savor the years
As life is not a race but a quest to live your best.
Reflect on and appreciate bygone days with gladness and glee,
And think of your blessings as healthy leaves on a tree.
Embrace what's before you one day at a time;
Encircle earthly splendor and give thanks to our heavenly Father, as He is divine.
Birthdays are special and gifts from above;
A time for reflecting, celebrating, and sharing with those you love.
Enjoy this birthday gala and all that it brings;
Have faith the ensuing years will bring you peace and fulfill many of your dreams.
Birthday wishes from friend one and friend two;
Celebrate, as tonight is all about you.

Two score and one year you have been so wonderfully blessed; take time to ponder your lifestyle choices as not to digress.

Wishful thinking will not execute any of your plans; you must to be obedient and ask God for a helping hand.

Enjoy all positive opportunities available to you; realize you are capable of reaching your goals if you just follow through.

Never allow others to determine your fate; you can be in control of your life if you accept biblical principles as your mate.

Together with loved ones you can succeed, and if you trust in Jesus, He will meet all your daily needs.

You are special, and we love you without borders, and that you should never doubt; we are here to support you if you don't give up and drop out.

Once you decide that you want to make a positive life change, you will experience peace and joy and realize what you have gained.

Never doubt your potentials, your ambition and your focus maintain; this will guarantee your goals you will obtain.

Embrace the opportunities you have been given, as God keeps giving you chance after chance; now it's time for you to change your dance.

Chapter Two

Celebrating Marriage

Forty-five years of marriage with some ups and some downs,
But because of God's unmeasured grace He keeps us closely bound.
Oftentimes loving and joyful, and sometimes not; occasionally we've been angry enough to shout.
But our trust in His Word enabled us to always be obedient and work things out.
I am thankful for the many years, children and grandchildren we have together,
And it will be my pledge to not purposely ruffle your feathers.
Our lives have been so incredibly blessed, and for that we both can respectfully attest.
So whatever the future might hold, if we are true to His Word, we will reach the goal.
I really do love you and that will always be true;
I am happy to be your wife and thankful that God gave me to you.

It's been three years; my goodness, how time flies,
But it's your love and commitment that bind the ties.
Although your daughters contributed some of the glue,
The other components came from the two of you.
We are proud of you both and love you lots;
We were wondering have you considered adding another child to the "children pot"?

We share our life, children and grandchildren, but that's not what it's all about;
As I love you with children and I loved you without.
There is something about you that I cannot explain
And living without you would result in turmoil and pain.

I applaud and admire you for:
Your love and respect for each other.
Your respect for the institution of marriage.
Your respect for family and friends.
Your reverence for God and His infinite blessings.

We wish you joy and happiness as you travel the sacred journey of matrimony. Remember that the path to creating and maintaining a Christlike marriage is to cultivate the seed and embrace the fruit of the Spirit:

Love, Faithfulness, Gentleness, Goodness, Joy, Kindness, Longsuffering, Peace, and Self-control

Always acknowledge an omnipotent, omnipresent and omniscient God in your life choices, and establish biblical ethics in adhering to your marriage vows. Our prayer is that you enjoy many years of perpetual happiness.

Love of my life, man of my dreams,
Who would have thought my life would be so esteemed.
You have caused me much joy and a little pain,
But the years have been great, so I really can't complain.
Times of laughter, times of sadness,
But praying together carried us through times of madness.
God keeps blessing us with much more than our share,
So how can we not praise Him and help others their burdens to bear.
I thank Him for grace, mercy, and my life He molded;
But most of all I thank Him for being the keeper of my soul.

Chapter Three

Honoring Mothers

Motherhood is a gift from God and embraces a very unique bond. As your daughter, I love you because:
You made a choice to give me life.
You sacrificed to feed, clothe, love, and nurture me.
You disciplined and encouraged me.
You are my model as a daughter, sister, wife, mother, grandmother, and friend.
Your love is the glue that binds our family.
I can never repay you for spiritual and earthly gifts.
Because of you, I am. I love and miss you so much.
Mom, you will forever linger in my heart.

You are a mother-to-be, and that is such an enormous blessing,
To give life to a person is one of God's most wonderful lessons.
Motherhood is a challenge like no other, but it brings love without measures;
So enjoy this beautiful gift from God.

You will give birth to someone special whether a he or a she.
Look forward in anticipation with great joy and countless days of glee;
Expect warming bottles and diapers filled with poo-poo and pee-pee.
Sleepless nights you can surely expect,
But because of your love for this baby all this you will lovingly accept.
Always remember to shower lots of love on this little bundle of joy,
As this baby is your responsibility to love, nurture, and enjoy.

You have been blessed with daughters who are the joy of your life, the love of your heart;
You have been blessed to be the one chosen to give them a start.
You can rejoice when they are waxed and flying on their own,
And you are to be applauded for providing them a safe, happy, loving Christian home.

Granddaughters are extra special, and so are you;
You are the child of my heart and I love you through and through.
You are now entering motherhood, and I marvel at how time flies;

Chapter Three: Honoring Mothers

It seems only yesterday you were a little girl asking me why.
God has chosen to make you a parent and give you a bundle of joy;
This child is to love, behold, and not treat as a toy.
Your eyes will gaze upon this child with wonders unknown;
And you will be blessed from above with joys of your own.
This precious gift is to nurture, protect, and to God uplift;
Don't be disobedient and risk the removal of God's special gift.
Give thanks for His goodness and all that He does;
Remember that all your blessings come from above.

The expectancy of another child was received with surprise and much joy.
We were delighted and of course hopeful the baby arrives as a boy.
Being a male or female really doesn't matter;
We'll just be thankful s/he enters the world with its entire tatter,
And wait with joy for the sounds of pitter-patter.

We know the girls are on cloud nine and incredibly thrilled;
Mommy and Daddy have hearts overflowing with happiness and loved-filled.
Children are blessings from our Father above,

Given to cuddle, teach, and shower with love.
Embrace the months until baby arrives;
Get plenty of rest, nourishment, and lots of exercise.
Husband and daughters will help you survive
As you labor to increase the family from four to five.

Know that you are greatly loved as you move from slim to slightly plump;
Enjoy all the pampering as you recline and rest on your rump.
With a smile on your face and a contented heart,
Your family will take your orders to help you get a jump-start.
We are so proud of the two of you and that's a fact;
You both have and deserve our love, support, and a soft pat on the back.

Motherhood is a special bond and one of God's most beloved and precious gifts;
The rewards are unnumbered with treasures you don't want to miss.
Always be willing to love, listen, teach, and share;
Your children will love you and someday show they really care.
You have been chosen to love, nurture, and be very forgiving;
As mothering entails a strong commitment of caring and sometimes a little stressful living.
Forever be willing to train your children in tools of

strength, virtue and character building. Your children should be the joy of your soul and the love of your heart, And you should be thankful for the blessing of being chosen to give them a start.

Although I cannot be with you to participate in your baby shower celebration, you can be confident, that as always, I am with you in spirit. It is my hope that today is a day filled with love, joy and happiness. Be thankful there are individuals who care enough to celebrate this occasion with you, and care enough to shower your baby with gifts even before he/she enters this world. Remember, we love you and care about your well-being. Take care of yourself and baby. Welcome to motherhood.

A bundle of joy, so precious and oh, so sweet;
A blessing from God to love, cuddle and gently rock to sleep.
One of God's treasures you've been chosen to keep;
Responsible to love and nurture from head to feet.
God has blessed and entrusted you with one of His own;
This is an enormous delight and of wonders yet unknown.
Enjoy this great blessing and all that it brings;
Teach your child to always reverence God and respect His domain.

A baby is a gift from God, so precious and so very sweet.
A soul to nurture, protect, and sing lullabies
As they are gently held and rocked to a peaceful sleep.
We marvel as we watch them grow and develop before our wondrous eyes;
Wondering where the years went as we teach them to survive.
You have been blessed with someone to love and embrace
During their journey on earth to a heavenly place.
You will be blessed with joys of your own;
So watch over this child, as he is one of God's own.

WELCOME GRANDCHILDREN

We were pleasantly surprised when informed of your journey from there to here, and we awaited your arrival with feelings of joy and excitement. The creation of life is one of God's most precious and amazing miracles and such a blessing.

Our prayer is:

You make the journey from entry to departure as a God-fearing person. It is our belief that God has a purpose in entrusting your care to your parents. Their responsibility is to love and discipline you, because if you train a child in the way s/he should go, when he is old he will not depart from it (Proverbs 22.6). Your responsibility is to love and honor your father and mother that your days may be long upon the land that the Lord gives you (Exodus 20:12).

We desire active involvement in your pilgrimage from

Chapter Three: Honoring Mothers

childhood to adulthood. We wait with anticipation being in attendance at your graduations, wedding, and the birth of your children.

"Trust in the Lord with all your heart, and lean not on your own understanding; in all your ways acknowledge Him, and He shall direct your paths" (Proverbs 3:5-6). We welcome you with love and pray God keeps you in His loving care.

We awaited your conception and arrival with anticipation and glee.
Your sisters were so excited that from the beginning they added you to the family tree.
Your mommy may have been inwardly anxious, but outwardly she was elegant, calm,
And throughout her pregnancy she glowed like the sun.
Your daddy was all smiles of pleasure and delight
At the fact that he now has another girl to hug and kiss goodnight.
Now that you have arrived we are all happy that we waited for the surprise.
A boy or a girl, no one told and no one admitted they knew,
But we were all thankful the gender resulted in you.
You were loved from the beginning and you will be loved to the end;
It is such a wonderful blessing there are now five in the family blend.
You are precious, special and ever so blessed
That into a loving family you have been born.

Your devoted parents and beautiful, energetic and creative sisters
Excitedly welcomed you with open arms.
We are overjoyed at being your grandparents; we love you and wish you the very best.
We are so thankful that God placed you in our family nest.

Chapter Four

Honoring Fathers

Son/Brother/Father, of the myriad names you are known by, nothing can equate the smile and beautiful sound of Dad from your children. What feelings of infinite love, swollen with pride and the abundance of joy as the affection ripples deep within the inners of your soul. What a blessing to be a parent.

To the love of my heart, joy of my soul,
You are the half that makes me whole.
Remarkable father of our wonderful sons,
I treasure the life that we have begun.
Through times of sorrow and scores of fun,
You are the family's anchor through many a storm.
God joined us together to remain always as one, to honor, love and obey;
Presenting examples to our sons and grandchildren in a biblical way.
Fathers are an essential facet of making the family unique
And the other half that makes a child's life complete.

Your transformation from singleness to husband, daddy and granddaddy is much admired,
A joy to observe as you wear these hats with such reserve.

You continue to rejoice in blessings upon blessings. Your children/grandchildren are privileged and take pleasure in having you as their daddy /granddaddy. I am grateful that you treasure, respect, and enjoy your God-designed family role. You are truly the love of my life.

Being a "daddy" and "granddaddy" are privileges, honors, and blessings from God. Your role is an integral ingredient of family life as you are the other half that makes your child and grandchild's life complete. Your dedication to fatherhood is to be commended, and it's a joy to be a part of this family unit. The laughter of children is such a wonderful sound as it brings love and a joy that's not easily found. Of all the hats that you wear, fatherhood is second to none. Your commitment as a parent is a means of depositing memories into a safety bank whereby your children can make loving withdrawals for the rest of their lives.

Chapter Four: Celebrating Fathers

To the son of our hearts, father of our beautiful grandchildren,
You are the pride of our life, joy of our soul
And you've earned our respect in your parenting control.
Your love and commitment in your fatherly role,
Demonstrate lots of respect for the road you chose.
We pray for your guidance as you lead the way,
And ask God's blessings that you strive to obey
And rear your children in the biblical way.
Your contribution to your family unit is reflected in the love of your wife and children,
And revealed in the characters of your offsprings.

It's an honor to be a father; without your children's love and needing you, what would your life be and what would you do? Your children are special and special gifts from above, given to nurture, love, shower with kisses, and give plenty of hugs. They can be ever so proud that you are their daddy/granddaddy, and they wouldn't hesitate to shout it out loud. Enjoy this Father's Day and all the joy and delight that it brings, because in your children's eyes you are the king.

Chapter Five

Thanks

As we get busy doing the things that we do, we oftentimes forget to take time to say "thank you" to those individuals who make a positive difference in our lives.

I often think of you and how you have so graciously adopted our mother. I wanted you to know how much I appreciate you taking time to demonstrate your love for her. She thinks you and your husband are quite remarkable and always has such wonderful things to say about you and your parents.

She enjoys your phone calls and visits, and she appreciates the gifts you so freely give. In today's society, it is not often that we find younger women showing respect and concern toward our mature generation. You are unquestionably putting your Christianity into practice. I really believe that "if you train up a child" he/she will not depart from those teachings. Your parents taught you well. My mother is certainly blessed to have you as a Christian friend. I just wanted to give you "flowers" now so you know how appreciative I am for your kindness toward "our" mother. I will remember you and your family in my prayers.

I opened the mail, and what did I find
A pair of Liz Claiborne pink pants that are now mine.
They were laundered and pressed and looked just like new;
I was quite surprised to find my wish had come true.
And so with my pink shirt and now pants to match,
I am ready for a nice lunch as soon as I grab my hat.
A gift from my niece, she's so sweet and kind;
She's beautiful, smart and one of a kind.
So accept this small token as a "thank you" from me,
And I wish you success in all you strive to be.

Thanks for your thoughtfulness and all that you do. We absolutely enjoyed the Christmas performance, and the company created an even more pleasurable evening. We also thank you for remembering our anniversary, gathering our leaves, and offering to lend a helping hand in whatever the need. Friends like the two of you contribute in making this earthly home a more pleasurable place. I am thankful that God placed us in Lake Tahoe at the same time. He knew we needed you in our lives. Again, thanks for your kindness; we enjoy and value your friendship.

My hope is that this note finds you enjoying good health and looking forward to tomorrow. I just wanted to let you know that I received your brief letter with the enclosed birthday gift; thank you. It is always so uplift-

Chapter Five: Thanks

ing when loved ones remember your birthday, and I appreciate your thoughtfulness.

We came for a family wedding and an opportunity to visit with family and friends, but we were sprinkled with an added treat. You were such a wonderful host. You not only invited us over for drinks and a scrumptious spaghetti dinner, but we also had an enjoyable and fantastic interaction in our sharing of travels, ideas, and opinions on a range of topics. You went beyond by opening your warm, comfortable, beautiful home and made us feel as though we were part of your extended family. Your warmth and hospitality were very much appreciated and well overboard; for that, we say thank you and may God's blessings be upon you and your loved ones.

It was a joy to see that you and my sister-in-law have remained friends over the years and have been supportive of each other in confronting the challenges of everyday life – true friendship is a wonderful stance. It was also heartwarming and refreshing to hear you acknowledge that you know you have been truly blessed and willing to share what God has so graciously allowed you to accumulate.

What a wonderful feeling to socialize with someone from the same geographical area, as one feels some manner of kinship in the knowing and sharing of similarities of being raised and nurtured in the same region of California.

Again, thank you, and we welcome the chance to meet again and return the generosity whenever you are visiting in our area.

P.S. Thanks for your encouragement in moving forward with a project that has been placed on my "to do list" for many years.

I really appreciate your contributions in making my special day "special." Thank you for the beautiful plant, soup book, joining us for dinner at one of my favorite restaurants, and inviting me to lunch. I enjoy our chats and always feel encouraged afterwards. Friends such as the two of you are what brighten our days and make life a little more enjoyable. Thank you.

I hope your holidays were filled with joy, peace, and hope. We must appreciate the fact that we are blessed to be counted with the ones enjoying a reasonable portion of good health and material possessions.

This note is to say thank you for thinking of me. It's nice to know that the little things we do for others are appreciated and remembered. I started reading the books, and it lightened my heart and brought smiles to my face. You and your granddaughter are welcome to our "bed and breakfast" anytime the need arises.

Chapter Five: Thanks

Thanks for thinking of me. Take care of yourself, and know that there is a God who loves us more than we can ever comprehend. Just trust Him as He is in control of everything. You have really been blessed. God has given you a great talent, and I thank you for sharing "Alabama Rabbit" with us. I wish you future success, and I hope that in your plans you will create a narrative that entails a "story" to influence our youth to have a desire to live their lives according to biblical principles. Your booklet motivated me to continue moving forward with my writing projects. Again, thanks for such a delightful word picture illustration. The art work was also very eye-catching. Keep creating!

Thanks for including us in your circle of friends to hoot and holler at the viewing of Super Bowl XL. We came to share in the enjoyment of delicious refreshments and the opportunity for Christian fellowship, but we were also sprinkled with an additional treat. You were such wonderful host and hostess, and we had an enjoyable and fantastic evening. You went beyond and opened your charming home and made us feel as though we were part of your extended family. Your warmth and hospitality were very much appreciated, and for that we say thank you.

We arrived home safe, and although it was wonderful returning to my comfort zone, we really enjoyed the visit. We came to pay our respects to you and your siblings at your father and our uncle's celebration from his earthly home to his heavenly home. But it also provided an opportunity to become acquainted with unknown relatives, reacquainted with others, and greet those we had not seen for several years. You were such a wonderful host. You not only made us feel at home in such pleasant surroundings, but you also provided a scrumptious dinner, and our interaction with each other was relaxed, enjoyable, and trusting.

I realize that the time since your father's passing has been very challenging, and that the task before you will require discernment and lots of gentleness. Therefore, my prayer is that you shoulder the responsibilities with the decorum that your father knew you were capable of displaying. It is my belief that all of our life experiences prepare us for the cross we have to carry during our life journey. You have been chosen as the family anchor, and I have no doubt that you will assume this role with humility and keep the love flowing within the family circle.

Chapter Six

Holiday Celebrations

It was the holiday season and all seemed just right;
The sun had set and it was drawing towards night.
I gazed in awe and marveled at the beautiful sights
As all looked beautiful as I listened to melodies of delight.
Presents all wrapped with exquisite bows,
Placed under a tree of beauty that glowed.
The tree was all covered with treasured ornaments and dazzling lights,
Everything looked scenic, and it was such a beautiful night.
In the air were the pleasing aromas of cinnamon pine cones and hickory spices;
Main entrée prepared, pies smelling great and cakes lined up ready to bake.
This was the perfect time for a long and much needed break.
But a soft tug at my heart gave a gentle reminder something wasn't quite right.
I had piddled and paddled from early dawn and far past midnight

Without giving Christ, my Savior, the slightest of thought
And all I could think was that's not right.
So I bowed my knees, and closed my eyes,
And made a much needed and honest plea:

Forgive me, my Lord, for not thinking of thee.
You died for my sins, and now I am free.
The blood that You shed and Your death on the cross
Is the reason I live and my soul is not lost.
When the day comes to a close and it's night all around,
Let me be grateful and reflect on Your mercies and blessings abound.
When I open my eyes from a night of safe and peaceful sleep,
Let me never forget to give thanks and biblical doctrine to share and forever keep.
As we celebrate this holiday season and all that it brings,
I will remember to worship His birth, death, resurrection, and the sacrifices made by Christ the risen King.
Amen.

As you reflect on the measures of this year, remember to give thanks for God's unlimited and unwavering grace and mercy. As you celebrate **Christ**mas, enjoying loved ones and friends, and anticipating another year,

Chapter Six: Holiday Celebrations

let us not forget to honor and reverence Him, the creator and sustainer of all things. We wish you a blessed holiday season.

As I reminisce on the birth of Christ and give thanks for His grace and mercy, I also give thanks for the happiness you bring to my life each and every day. And although I can't express myself the way I would like, I will sum up all my deepest thoughts in these words: "I love you and am blessed to be your wife."

Because of His birth, death, and resurrection, we celebrate, embrace, and rejoice in:
Christianity
Holiness
Righteousness
Inspiration
Salvation
Trinity
Messiah
Anointed
Scripture
Give thanks for years past and look forward with anticipation to the coming year.

Merry Christmas! We hope that Santa, Mommy, and Daddy remembered that you were a very good and responsible daughter and sister this past year. We miss being with you this Christmas, but we wish you lots of love. Enjoy all of your gifts and we hope to see you soon. Hugs and Kisses.

Merry Christmas! We hope that Santa was very nice to you because you have been such a good little girl. You help Mommy, and you always play with Daddy and big sister. We love you very much and hope to see you soon.

The year is ending, and Santa said it's been a rough year,
So here's something we hope will bring you a little cheer.
Spend it with care to make it last,
As your grandpa and grandma are not made out of cash.
Enjoy this Christmas and all that it brings,
But always remember we are celebrating the birth of Christ the King.

You are my sister; that's such a remarkable blessing, and I think that's really great,
So during this Christmas season, remember to rejoice and celebrate.
This small gift is given with love from our hearts,

Chapter Six: Holiday Celebrations

To get your holiday shopping off to a good start.
As you celebrate this holiday season and all that it brings,
Remember to worship the birth and sacrifices of Christ our King.

As we quietly close the door on the past year, as we reminisce on another year of unmerited blessings, as we look forward to the coming year, remember from whom all blessings flow. Remember to rejoice and give thanks for His goodness, and celebrate His birth, death, and resurrection.

Blessings after blessings He keeps giving us more,
Because of His sacrifices we have access through the heavenly door.
I am blessed to have been joined to you and that makes us one;
I have faith that we have been chosen and there is work to be done.
United we worship Him, His birth, death, and rebirth;
Unwavering in our thankfulness of a blessed life on this earth.
As we gently close the door on this year and cross the threshold into the coming year, let us not resist
That Jesus Christ is the reason we celebrate and that we all exist.

Santa said you have been a good little boy,
And we think that's very nice.
So we told your Mom to buy you some noisy toys;
Something that goes clang-clang and ends with a big bang.
After awhile you will be ready for a long nap
And she will plop down and give a big clap.

Because He rose Easter is a time of reflecting, rejoicings, and praising. Reflect on His renowned sacrifices. Rejoice on His birth/crucifixion/resurrection. Happy Easter – reverence this time of remembrance!

Chapter Seven

Graduation Celebrations

A day to remember, cherish, and respect;
Bygone days filled with fun and a few regrets.
Great memories, friends, teachers, and loads of fun,
Regrets, not many, but they are not for reruns.
Great years are for reflection, although sometimes not quite so easy to digest;
Days of unforgettable activities during lunch and recess.
Useful info to retain toward a degree we hope you endeavor to obtain.
Attitude, attitude of that you lack none,
But respectful and appreciative you have finally become.
Total commitment and dedication with a heart full of love;
Insightful, not always, but thankful for blessings from above.
Only by God's grace are you so wonderfully blessed;
Not only your obedience allowed you to endure the test.
But parents, grandparents, and family encouraged you to always strive for the best.

We are extremely proud of you and wish you lots of success.

Congratulations as you optimistically close the door of high school and gallantly open the door of higher education. As you embark upon the pathway of adulthood, we wish you wisdom in making intelligent decisions, choosing an admirable career, and being cautious in your selection of friends and associates. Be persistently mindful of your heritage, and remember, in all your ways acknowledge God and allow Him to direct your lifestyle choices.

You have earned the privilege to modestly boast in your accomplishments. But always give recognition and thanks to Christ, the One who "crowned your head with wisdom and knowledge." Your parents, family, and friends have reason to be proud, and so do you. Be mindful that not only your determination allowed you to endure adversity, but those who love and care about you prayed and encouraged you to always endeavor to do your best.

Chapter Eight

An Assortment of Poems

We welcome you, our new daughter-in-law, into our family with love and affection. We envision and look with anticipation to a delightful and warm-hearted relationship. Our desire is to be in-laws that are kind-hearted, supportive, and approachable without being intrusive. We value and respect your choices as you and your daughter merge and become an integral part of our family.

May the spirit of Christ forever dwell in the crevices of your heart and earthly home
May those who enter feel His unwavering love emanating from your spirit
May biblical doctrine forever be the cornerstone and pinnacle of home activities
May you forever believe that because He died and rose, you are now assured a heavenly home.
God bless this home.

We came for the funeral, which was a sorrowful occasion, but we enjoyed seeing family and friends and had a great time. Since returning home you have been constantly on my mind. I am glad we took pictures in which you look just great, so I am sending them to you as a personal keepsake. Place them in an area so visitors can see, and I want you to know you are still quite beautiful to me.

We are all family; God planned and designed it so;
Therefore we must be forgiving and loving if we are to grow.
To keep each other updated concerning the family tree,
I have compiled a condensed history to turn the key.
Each of us must be committed and have a role to play,
But you must be agreeable to assist in some significant way.
When you are part of a new life entering this world,
Share with the family if it's a handsome boy or beautiful girl.
We must all take a pledge to keep each other informed;
Promise to pray for each other and embrace family concerns
As I believe that's how strong and loving families are formed.

Sisters, the contents of this gift were assembled with love and given from the heart;

Chapter Eight: An Assortment of Poems

I am hopeful this will be a new beginning for a united family start.
If there are inaccuracies or omissions contained within,
Charge them to my forgetfulness and not my heart as a sin.
Make the revisions and let us all know;
So that as a family we will share and continue to grow.
We are a family, and I think that's a blessing and incredibly nice;
But my prayer is that someday soon we are all united in Jesus Christ.

We are happy for you and delighted that you've moved into your new home;
Carve out some personal time as to the stores you must roam.
We know that you are blessed and will give thanks prior to putting down stakes,
And we give this plant with hope the roots germinate and growth will begin to take.
We present this gift as our token of friendship and agape love,
Hoping it thrives as you receive blessings from above.
Remember, a house is not a home
Until you invite God's spirit in every room to dwell and roam.

We are discovering you to be a conscientious individual, refined, and possessing admirable character traits. We welcome you as the wife of our son and the mother of our future grandchildren.

Oh how I love you, let me count the ways.
Be assured there are many more, but I'll save them for other days:
    You are allowing God to order your steps.
    You are the half that makes me whole.
    You are the father of my children.
    You are who you are.
    You love me.

You are leaving JEM church family and moving away;
That makes us all sad in our own special way.
We enjoyed you both in our DPL group
As you have a great sense of humor and made us all laugh and hoot.
Your husband is quiet and seemed somewhat reserved;
We wish him success as he does speak when he conquers his nerves.
We wish you God's grace and also His speed;
We pray that you continue doing mission and ministry deeds.
We will miss your great smiles and your positive attitudes;
As you always appeared in an upbeat mood.

Chapter Eight: An Assortment of Poems

We pray for your strength as you parent your sons;
Don't ever forget they are blessings from God, and they are also His sons.
We pray for your trust in Jesus our Lord,
As believing and obeying will keep you onboard.
Whenever you are in the valley and it seems like no one really cares;
Remember the One who loves you and your burdens He shares.
Trust in His Word and never doubt because
You can be assured that whatever the storm He is with you and will bring you out.

Welcome to the "Family."
You have joined the Church Family and we think that's awesome and really great;
We Christians rejoice, but the devil is full of anger and hate.
Day by day remember to pray, read, study and obey.
Hold fast to God's Word; this will keep you faithful and onboard.
The world is full of transgression, bitterness and disarray,
But we must believe His Word will pave the way,
So trust Him to guide you as He looks down from above.
Have faith and allow Him to guide you when trying to decide;
Remember when we are praying Jesus is working on the other side.

I enjoyed your presentation at our Women's Day program. Although you are a novice speaker, your subject matter was overflowing with substance that was biblically based, and your delivery was awesome. You are now "out of the boat and walking on water." Refuse to set limits on yourself, and do not waver in allowing God to increase your boundaries by providing opportunities to share His Word. If you trust Him, He will give you the courage and determination to accomplish your mission, for which you were fashioned before your birth. Persevere in giving Him all the glory and all the praise.

You are stylishly slender and fashionably tall,
But hold on for a minute, because that is not all.
Your stride is graceful and your attire is always so incredibly tasteful.
You made a decision your life to revive;
I wish you success and have faith that you will survive.
Time spent knowing you have been really great
And I wish you blessings on this journey you chose to partake.
I will miss seeing you on our unofficial Sunday dates,
Although you always manage to arrive somewhat late.
You are our sister in Christ, and we wish you well,
So keep in touch and let us know you and family are doing swell.
We came to dinner to show we care,

Chapter Eight: An Assortment of Poems

And will remember you and your children in our prayers.

Over the years we embraced the force of giving thanks for the evolving of treasured friends. Each of you populates this arena of friendship. We remember times shared over dinners, phone conversations, and impromptu visits with family and friends that bring reflections of joyful memories. We appreciate your integrity and simplistic life application, and we count it a blessing to be included in your realm of friends. Although our friendship is a novice relationship, our solidarity increases as we share measures of triumphs and encumbrances that God allows to enhance our spiritual growth. Reflecting on myriad similarities in our Christian beliefs and espouse in family values, we look forward to many years of unwavering friendship.

Friendship, what a wonderful stance; you welcomed old neighbors and friends without a backward glance. We came for our family reunion, a tour of New Orleans, and a popcorn visit to our friends in Slidell; but we were in for a treat, as you were such wonderful hostess we have considered Slidell the place we should dwell. You opened your home and welcomed us to room and board; your warmth and hospitality were very much appreciated and well overboard. You served tasty chicken wings and made scrumptious gumbo that was fit for queens and kings. We enjoyed stimulating conversation and a fantastic lake view; we welcome the chance to began anew and return this generosity to the two of you. We really enjoyed spending time with you, meeting your niece, and the tour of the housing development was also a nice venue. You have a beautiful home, and it was so refreshing to hear you acknowledge that you know all you possess is because you are truly blessed.

We met for dinner as Christians to celebrate, and we formed a group that totaled ten; now the two of you are leaving, and that's not an easy thing for us to take. We respect your decision, are happy for you, and think it's really great. We'll miss your faces and pleasant attitudes, but we will remember you with care; we'll pray for God's covering, His love, and teachings you will generously share. Forever trust Him - hold fast to His principles - allow Him to lead; you will be blessed, and He will meet all your emotional and spiritual needs.

Out in the Mississippi Gulf, adjacent to New Orleans,
The winds were intense and the waters were unsettled and quite extreme.
The tempest increased its tempo and arrived upon shore,
Provoking a disturbance on the Pontchartrain Lake floor;
Resulting in the overflow of its banks and penetrating

your front door.
Katrina 2005 was ferocious, causing the waters to rise extremely high,
And many began praying to our heavenly Father in the sky.
Katrina attempted to devour all life form, material possessions and consume the land, but could not succeed because God is in complete control and had another plan.

He has a plan for your life in which you must take a stand,
To embrace His teachings and bow down to no other god or man.
Life is a precious gift, and He holds it in the palm of His hands,
You are to believe on His promise, obey His commands,
Praise His name and boldly stand.

Your life has been spared to praise His name,
Forsaking all others and material gains.
You receive His blessings without selfish pride,
Refusing to allow earthly possessions to shove family and friends aside.
You honor Him by generously giving back
And refrain from soliciting accolades or pats on the back.

His blessings are unnumbered and unwavering day after day.

You cannot allow yourself to falter in honoring Him when you pray.
Ask Him to forgive you and your life to mold
And that He is the eternal keeper of your soul.
We pray for God's blessing upon your home

Etiquette ('e-ti-kit / ket)

Etiquette, etiquette striving to enhance and much more;
So we aren't reluctant and hesitant in entering the door.
A fundamental social attribute which everyone needs;
Unfamiliarity and being uninformed shouldn't humiliate or bend our knees.
Learn all the skills you can and be perceptive of the rest;
So when the occasion arises you'll be prepared to endure the test.
Learning the essentials is easy as making mud pies;
But trying to remember all the rules will surely bring tears to anyone's eyes.
Listed are a few agreed upon rules that's useful to know
Prior to entertaining or going out to eat;
They are easy to remember and can change
An unpleasant situation to something that's really quite neat.

Chapter Eight: An Assortment of Poems

Without A Doubt
Look all around you, and what do you see?
A world filled with chaos in the air, on land, and at sea.
Life is a challenge, and that's a known fact,
but there are Christian values you must embrace to keep the devil off your back.
If the ladder you're climbing is unsteady and leaning against a crumbling wall,
That's a sure sign things are out of order and you're headed for a great fall.
Climb down from that unbalanced ladder and make a u-turn;
God will provide loved ones and angels to guide you and be the wind beneath your arms.
If your life is in turmoil and you're feeling discouraged and can't see your way out,
Remember that God is always present and that you don't have to doubt.
There is no need to despair, become frightened and allow the devil to have his way;
When negative feelings overtake you, just think of God's goodness and pray.
He will guide and protect you and ease your pain,
If only you trust Him, your life will never be the same.
Bid farewell to immoral friendships or your life will not gel;
Your soul will be lost and spend eternity in hell.
The devil's job is to kill, steal, and destroy
And he is using all his weapons as that is his ploy.
He's working overtime to draw you in
And continually striving to crush you so he can win.
If you are associating with negative friends trying to drag you down,

Refuse their offer and let them know you're turning your life around.
Invite them to join you on your quest for a new life
And to partner with you as you strive daily to live for Jesus Christ.
Always remember there are people who love you, people who care;
So don't approach life on some double-dare.
There are people waiting to help you when life seems unkind and unfair.
There are people offering up prayers, extending a helping hand
And ready to assist in your Christian stand.
God is merciful and you have been wonderfully blessed,
So don't waste your remaining years on the devil's mess;
Make a decision today to obey biblical principles and give God your best.
Your rewards will be immeasurable, but not always carefree.
You will enjoy burst of sunshine and encounter some rain,
But you can be assured your soul will be safe with Jesus who is in control of all things.
Remember, tomorrow is not promised so why take a chance?
Ask Christ to order your steps and you will be taking the right stance.
Suggestion: *Every day read a chapter in the book of Proverbs as it has the answers to all your questions for godly living. Before and after reading, pray for understanding and ask God to direct your life.*

Chapter Nine

Tributes

A Tribute to My Parents

Have I told you lately that I love you, have I told you how much I care,
You are my life inspiration and I really do care.
As I sit and stare out the window thoughts of you are everywhere,
You are in my subconscious and you will forever dwell there.
When I look at my surroundings and cannot find you anywhere,
In my heart I feel the emptiness and remember how much you cared.
Your love and words of wisdom will always be my guiding light
And I will forever remember your teachings as I persevere and live this mortal life.
Your trust in God molded my life decisions and channeled my belief in Christ.
When I count my blessings, many answered because of your constant prayers;

I give thanks and lift my eyes toward heaven, knowing you are rejoicing there.
You may not have been perfect, but in you I found no designed imperfection,
You were my parents and I loved you without doubt or exception.
Oftentimes I neglected to share my deepest feelings and I will forever have regrets,
But oh how I miss your presence, and in my heart you hold a place never to forget.
I didn't often tell you how much your were loved, cherished and respected,
But because of your biblical teachings, I am now Spirit-filled and Christ connected.

Have you told anyone lately that you love them?
Have you told anyone lately how much you care?
Don't squander the time that's now before you;
Tell loved ones that you love them and that you truly do care.

A Tribute to My Husband

Often I reflect on the first time ever I saw your face, my imaginativeness never reached the depth of what God had planned for our shared lives.

Since becoming your wife and the mother of your children, I have experienced joy, peace, and happiness beyond my subliminal imagination.

Constant my prayer requests are longevity with you and giving thanks to God for choosing me as your "rib mate."

Although I possess the propensity of sheltering my inner feelings, be assured the small inner voice loudly proclaims, "I love you, I love you, I love you."

Remembering the past, appreciative of the present, and anticipating many years of togetherness, my desire is that you always be mindful that you are not only my best friend, but also the love of my life.

A Tribute to Our Sons
You are:
Outstanding in your personality and the type of son any parent would be proud to acknowledge.
Sensitive and nourishing, and we are elated for the opportunity of being involved as you made the journey from stages of infancy into fatherhood and grandfather.
Caring and committed to your role as son, brother, father, grandfather, and you embrace these responsibilities with love and affection.
Appreciative of life's blessings and cognizant of the importance of family unity.
Responsible and an individual who acquired and developed interests that are sound in judgment. We have compassion for your personal life choices and embrace your career choices. We are grateful for having had the responsibility of nurturing and protecting you, and thankful that God chose us to be your parents.
We love you.

You are:
Kindhearted in your personality traits and the type of son any parent would be proud to acknowledge.
Enjoyable in your interactions, and we are elated for the opportunity of being involved as you matured from infancy, manhood, husband, and fatherhood.
Nourishing in the hue of society and a positive role model to young men.

Joyful in your role of son, brother, uncle, husband, and father and appreciative of the importance of family unity.

Ingenious in your quest to acquire, develop, and maintain interests that are sound in judgment. We espouse the confidence you have embraced in your personal and career choices.

We are grateful for having had the responsibility of nurturing and protecting you, and thankful that God chose us to be your parents.

We love you.

A Tribute to Pastor and Wife

They are committed Christian soldiers, steadfast in their praying and striving daily to live their life for Jesus Christ. They are positive and encouraging, and such a wonder of delight; they are devoted to the Jubilare Family, never seeking recognition or the limelight. They boldly walk the life they teach and talk about and will not hesitate to sometimes sing or loudly shout it out.

As a shepherd there are many trials and tribulations that they must endure, providing insight and perception so that in their Christian life they soar. They are determined to be ever truthful and faithful to their Christian calling, teaching, and counseling the flock to impede their spiritual falling. God has blessed and given Pastor a Christian vision; therefore, it's our spiritual duty to be cohesive and not cause discord or division. God has placed him as Shepard over the Jubilare

Evangelistic Ministries flock; we are to be obedient and not become stumbling blocks.

This earthly journey is not easy, nor did they expect that it would be. But they embraced their Christian duty, ministering to others so they might see that being obedient to biblical doctrine encompasses all that's needed to be spiritually free.

Family and children calling, Honey "do list" to complete, and sometimes golfing with the boys, yet allowing time to play with the grandchildren and their many, many toys. Sunday service, Wednesday night Bible study, and other weekday chores leave little time for self-indulgence or even think of being bored.

We, as members, often present with a little of this and a lot of that, forgetting that occasionally they need a "thank you" and a soft, gentle pat on their backs. We are very grateful to God for sending them our way; therefore, we are expressing our appreciation and honoring them on this designated day. Be assured that the Jubilare family loves you and we genuinely do care; we are thankful to your family for their unselfishness and willingness to share. We are blessed that you are our shepherd and our burdens you help to bear; for this and other contributions, we thank God and remember you in prayer.

You are true believers of the promise that eternal life is a guarantee; you will suffer no more pain, no more sorrow, no need to stay on bended knees. You are strong and graceful branches, bearing good and healthy fruit; you are tolerant and faithful to the church family group. You have Jesus Christ's assurance that when your time on earth is ended, you will both be holy branches on the celestial Living Tree.

Chapter Nine: Tributes

Retirement

She awakened this morning and eased out of bed, said her prayer and held her head; thought for a moment, and realized she was retired so she eased back into bed. She read her Bible, gave thanks for her sins Christ died, and therefore blessed and spiritually alive. She cautiously jumped out of bed and gave a jubilant hoot, thanking God for a new day and the blessings of retiring with enough loot.

She pondered the duties of a respectful, submissive, dutiful and obedient wife, and after some thought, reached the conclusion that retirement indeed was rather nice. With a smile on her face she proceeded to do laundry, ironed, cleaned, and planned weekly meals to cook, and having extra time, she relaxed and read one of her many self-help books.

She adorned the table with fine linen, china and silver, lit the candles and dimmed the lights, thinking life is so wonderful and retirement is such a grand delight. She beautified herself and anxiously awaited her husband's evening arrival, and when he entered the door his heart fluttered at her beauty and retirement survival. He was in such awe at her high spirits and quite taken, as the look about her was so serene that he pinched himself as he thought he surely must be revisiting last night's dream.

The conversation was delightful, dinner delicious and very, very nice as they feasted on salad, chicken, mustard greens, cornbread, and shrimp served on a bed of rice. He had longed for this type of day-to-day life with his wife who's beautiful, talented, and oh so nice.

So whatever her desires, he is more than willing to give, just don't expect him to be at her beck and call and turn cart wheels.

Remembering you for:

Influencing not only our youth, but the church family by the presence of a positive attitude and your unwavering Christian faith.

Nurturing our youth to improve their performance in academics and symbolizing a persuasive force in channeling their preference in attending an institution of higher learning.

Spiritual behavior revealed in interactions with homeless individuals, persons confined to assisted-living residences, and others encountered on your earthly journey.

Perseverance as you embraced a Christian lifestyle with commitment and strength of mind in the acknowledgment of divine submission.

Instrumental in the formation and administration of the church's tutoring program; also coaching, supporting, and encouraging myriad youth in their comprehension of scholastic assignments and elevating educational proficiency.

Rejoicing in the Lord, and your spiritual growth obtained from reading, studying, and sharing Scripture and your tenacity for being obedient to God's Word.

Attributes and character traits displayed that are admirable, ethical and give credence to your Christian walk.

Chapter Nine: Tributes

Trusting in biblical doctrine to weave threads to fashion the fabric of your soul and provide assurance of everlasting life.

Innovation in the motivation of our youth to bring awareness to their potentials and the desire to strengthen, expand their horizons, and reach their aspirations.

Optimism in your passion to be a faithful servant for Christ and enthusiastically serving others.

Noblility in rejecting worldly pleasures, denial of self, and giving God all praise and all glory.

Chapter Ten

Praises of Jubilare

In our first year at Jubilare we worshiped in Pastor and Sis. Walton's garage
Praying, singing, and giving praises to our merciful and ever-loving God.

In our second through sixth years at Jubilare we worshiped in rental space
Praying, singing, and giving praises for His immeasurable grace.

In our seventh year at Jubilare God blessed us with a beautiful sanctuary
Praying, singing, and giving praises for His blessings of not being stubborn and contrary.

In our eighth year at Jubilare God's love and blessings continued to astound
Praying, singing, determined to remain faithful and heaven bound.

In our ninth and tenth years at Jubilare we continued to rejoice and praise His holy name
Thankful to God for sending His Son and accepting us into His sacred domain.

In our eleventh year at Jubilare we were blessed to purchase additional space
Thankful for God's goodness, kindness, and His unlimited grace.

It's our twelfth year at Jubilare; we celebrated and continued to honor His holy name
Truthfully dividing His Word and all our transgressions to refrain.

In our thirteenth year at Jubilare we are triumphant and filled with glee
Never forgetting to be thankful by staying on bended knees.

We are striving always to obey Him, crushing our arrogance and our pride.
We have faith that when we are praying, God is working on the other side.
We are confident that when this earthy life is over, with Him we will reside.

frm-lph

Chapter Eleven

Sympathy

I offered up a prayer for you after you shared the passing of your dear grandmother from her earthly home. But because of her belief in Christ, you can have peace of her final resting place.

You have the memories of all the love and care you showered upon her during her earthly journey. Always remember that nothing can take from you the wealth of information, spiritual values, wonderful memories, and happiness that your grandmother shared with you and other loved ones for so many years.

Although we don't understand why those we love are taken when we are not prepared to "let go and let God have control," we can be assured that God, who is the giver, sustainer, and taker of life, is in complete control.

Continue to trust Him to order your steps, and He will provide the comfort needed as you travel through this time of sorrow.

We were sorry to hear of your father's passing from this world, although because of his belief, you can have peace of his final destination. Our prayers and sympathies go out to you and your family for your loss.

Chapter Twelve

Remembering Birthdays

You are blessed to be celebrating year sixty-nine, and I am so thankful to be yours and assured that you are mine. Years of reflecting on how blessed you are; experiencing a few trials and a little strife, but there is comfort in being loved by and belonging to Jesus Christ.

Enjoy this enormous blessing and the year ahead; remembering always to be persistent in God's stead. He blessed you with a wife who really loves you including children and grandchildren that feel that way too. We all think you are devoted to family and super great, and pray we are all united behind the Pearly Gates.

Birthdays, a time to appreciate, a time to savor and moments of reflecting; you can be sure your special day we would never think of neglecting. We deliver birthday wishes from Mom and Dad; your husband and daughters are blessed to have you, a person with a persona many wish they had. We love and admire you, pleased that you are a member of our family group, and would not trade you as our daughter-in-law even if there were a family coup. Soul-mate of our son and giver of life to our granddaughters, nope, we would not even consider trading you for a slot machine full of quarters. Today is your birthday, relax and enjoy; allow others to pamper you and receive this gift with love and joy.

You hail from San Francisco, standing over six feet tall, shaved your head which rendered you bald. Your wife really does not care as she loves with or without hair, and confident that with God's blessing the two of you will always be a pair. You are celebrating birthday sixty-two and we think that's really neat, and enjoy times together sharing something delicious to eat. It is nice to have met and formed a friendship with you two, and our lives are enriched since meeting both of you. Things that are said and things that we do leave us with the assurance we can rely on you. We hope this birthday brings you happiness and joy, and you gave thanks for the blessings you daily enjoy. Accept this birthday wish from friend one and friend two; know there is a place in our hearts for the two of you.

Chapter Twelve: Remembering Birthdays

Happy birthday to a loveable and fantastic son; we feel blessed for the gift of being your parents, and thankful that you are confident in:
Knowing who you are
Being who you are
Accepting who you are
Remember, birthdays are special and gifts from above, so give God thanks and show Him love.

You may have slammed the door on eleven and bravely opened the door to twelve, but we know that deep within your heart is beginning to swell. Now that you are twelve and on the path to becoming a teen, there are a few tips you must always remember if you want to be successful and keen:
Respect, trust and obey Mom and Pops as they love you a lot
Be careful in your peer selections as they can be deceptive and loaded with schemes and plots
Be aware of who you are and don't allow aliens to decide
Your parents, sisters and grandparents love you and will always be by your side
You are on your way to being a teen and that's a blessing and really great, but remember to always be very careful of the daily choices you must make. You may have bid a soft farewell to eleven and loudly yelled hello to twelve, but we know that as you stepped in the door your heart began to swell. You are noticeably charming and somewhat smart, and although you are aware

of that, it's really not bragging, just a small known fact.
This is a special day and all that it brings
You are rather cute, have a friendly personality and deserve nice things
You sing, dance, write stories, and aware of the latest teen fashion trends
Get ready to celebrate this twelfth birthday with family and friends
Remember at the end of the day this special treatment comes to an end.

You have reached the age of sixty plus two and we must confess the years look rather handsome on you. Although thinning, you managed to retain some hair, decorum of flair and on Sunday mornings you are able to lift your hands in the air. We share this birthday celebration with gladness and glee, knowing at times all of us experience aches, pains and weakness in our knees. Only God's blessings brought you this far, so do not allow life's scars to alter your path or cause you mar. Don't permit numbers to get you down or turn that smile into a frown. You are blessed in the midst of this earthly mess, but rejoice because when you depart you will enjoy eternal rest. Although it's sometimes difficult to accept that you can no longer sprint with speed or catch that football pass, but you know only what you do for Christ will last. There really is no need to fret about climbing another birthday hill, just keep still and, as needed, take a prayer pill.

Chapter Twelve: Remembering Birthdays

Birthdays, birthdays what a great blessing and wonderful treat; so don't allow the elevated number to bring dismay or be the cause of you wanting to retreat. You are blessed to be surrounded by family and friends, people who love you a lot, and wouldn't trade you for the Florida lottery pot. We hope this occasion results in wonders beyond belief as you celebrate and turn another "birthday year" leaf. We love you as sister, sister-in-law and friend, and the various things we continue to share are treasured and instilled deep within. We are sending birthday wishes from us two, and want you to know that our family wouldn't be the same if it didn't include you.

Chapter Thirteen

Magnificent — Marriage Moments

Love, commitment and forgiveness are main ingredients in the Marriage Cake, but it is crucial that you mix in oodles of giving, forgiving and just a pinch of take; bend all components together and the batter is ready to bake. Guard the Marriage Cake closely and don't allow temperatures to rise, issues to simmer or pile extremely high. If you ignore these instructions your Marriage Cake will fall and you will be deprived of a long-lasting marriage wall. You must place family, friends and others on the back burner and cling to each other through frosty winters and blistering summers. Forsaking all others must be the primary plan if you want your marriage to endure into eternity land. *(Matthew 19:5)*
We are quite proud of you two, the family things that you do and encouraging your daughters to be well-mannered, kindhearted and true. Marriage is not stress-free, we know that is an absolute fact; but remain faithful by having each others back. We all make mistakes

as we boldly stand and meet life challenges in this hostile land. Marriage brings a wealth of pleasure and of course some rain, but through it all God continues to reign. No matter what comes, no matter what the blunder, always remember what God joined together let no one put asunder (*Matthew 19:6*).

We are celebrating forty-six years of marriage with countless smiles; encountered our share of day-to-day and diverse trials. We shared some tears and also some frowns, and from time-to-time we both behaved immaturely, acting like clowns. But, as I reawaken memories of all we have been through, I am blessed to have traveled this journey with you. You add deeply to my happiness and the joy of my life, and a life without you I will not sacrifice. Blessed am I to be married to you, and I am so appreciative for who you are and all that you do.

Chapter Fourteen

Congratulations

We are confident the theatrical production was a great success, and you did your best in the role you were chosen to recreate. I think it's wonderful that you auditioned, selected as a cast member and performed magnificently. Your parents are so proud of you and delighted that, not only were they able to attend the showing but, your sister and cousins were also there for support. We wait with excitement to hear them recount the details, and hopefully we will be able to attend a future presentation. Continue to trust Him, as when one door closes, it's just an opportunity for God to open another "blessing door" in your life.

I acknowledge that my "Great Job" is slightly late, but did not want the opportunity to slip by without offering my congratulations. You, and your family, can be proud of your accomplishments. You not only juggled family, job and school responsibilities, you refused to be neglectful in allowing time in your busy schedule to give praise and honor to God. You can also be thankful that you realize He is the One who provided the fortitude to pursue higher education, yet refusing to put educational goals ahead of serving Him. I am delighted for the opportunity of becoming acquainted with you, and it is always pleasant to greet you as your countenance seems to consistently reflect joyfulness.

You are blessed to be raised by parents that not only love you, but parents that believe in and live by biblical principles. Your bible study presentation was delivered in a very proficient manner, as not only did you display fortitude in presenting before your peers and the congregation, you were focused and spoke truth boldly. Your spirit and mannerism mirrored that you believed and understood how this portion of scripture, depicting David's reliance on God, relates to the issues we stumble upon in our daily interactions. In my observation of you, it appears you emulate what I believe your parents are teaching at home, and living as an example to their children and others they encounter. Continue standing boldly for Christ, thereby being a role model to others. Allow Him to order your steps, and you will face the seasons of difficulties with assurance that "with God all things are possible". You are a young lady your parents can be proud to call daughter.

Albeit, a visit to the dental office is not high on our list of "most enjoyable things to do", but visits are more pleasant because of you. Be assured the entire staff is courteous in their interactions, but you exude cheerfulness and perpetually make us feel as though our satisfaction is of great concern. I have observed you dealing with patients and clients in person and by phone, and you repeatedly exhibit a professional, yet friendly demeanor in your verbal and non-verbal responses. You appear to be blessed with the gift of making an individual feel "at home" even though you may be wishing that individual was "at home". Although we all have personal challenges, you seem to balance your personal life and professional life in a way that allow God's blessings to radiate through you onto others. Whenever we call or present in the office, you are affable and seem to make every effort to accommodate our needs. You are a jewel as front office coordinator/manager. We are confident your employers are acquainted with and acknowledge your professional qualities and that your mannerism contributes significantly to the opinions formed by individuals entering the office.

CHAPTER FIFTEEN

Meaningful Sharings

Although this "thank you" note is slightly late, but you must sympathize with us as we were in Los Cabos enjoying a much deserved break. We really appreciated your spontaneous brunch invitation to the group; the gathering of these eight individuals is a somewhat indescribable troupe. You guys are such hospitable hosts, that sometimes you must boldly open the door and tell us it's time to adios.

We, the group, were invited to your home for dinner long at last, and happily looked forward to the fellowship and knew we would, as usual, enjoy each others company and have a blast. We so thoroughly enjoyed the Cornish hens that we would seriously consider rearranging our schedules and accepting an invitation to come for dinner again. We were served yummy lemon cake that was so delicious everyone was tempted to smack their lips and lick their plates. The cheesecake was brand-named, scrumptious, room temperature and not cold. You can believe that in the future when speaking of your cooking we will say nice things and be outrageously bold.

Chapter Sixteen

Soothing Your Sorrows

We experience loneliness after the death of a loved one and the passing of your brother is sure to leave an emptiness not only in the life of his twin sister, but also in the life of other loved ones and friends. Commit to memory the joyful childhood experiences and other happy events to keep his memory imprinted on your heart. Allow your faith in God to give you peace now and in the days to come. We, your friends, are thinking of you and empathize with you in this time of loss.

Although we realize the days on earth are predestined for each of us and, yes, maybe we believe the individual is in a healthier place but, yet and still, the departing of a loved one is sometimes difficult to embrace. Know that we care about you; therefore we are compassionate about the things that affect you and your family. In remembering, revel in the wonderful and inspiring conversations the two of you shared. Reflect on the tidbits of information imparted that you are now putting into practice, and the values that you embrace and convey as you interact with others. Just treasure the memories.

My hope is that this note finds you recuperating with increased swiftness. We know God is working to heal both the internal and external facets of your being; therefore, you can praise Him and continually give thanks that you recognize the value of who He is. We miss your presence during Sunday worship, and wanted to let you know that you are thought of often and remembered in our prayers. I think it's always uplifting when sisters-in-Christ remember each other, so take joy my "sister" that you are remembered.

Our prayers include not only a swift healing, but that you remember God is sustaining you in His graces. We often times wonder "why did this happen to me", but be assured that although things appear to be dismal, your misfortune provided your sisters-in-Christ an opportunity to put their beliefs into action by doing for you. So revisit your "falling down the stairs" as your church sisters "walking up the stairs" to fulfill one of their assigned duties which is caring for each other. Use this time to read, study and apply His Word by allowing Him to direct your steps and don't allow Satan to

Chapter Sixteen: Soothing Your Sorrows

deprive you of God's blessings. Although you are not able to participate in your chosen ministry, you can minister to others as they stop by to assist you. You can demonstrate to visitors that your decrease in mobility only increased your faith that God is in control of your life and you will continue to give Him all honor and all praise. I hope this basket of fruit nourishes your body with each nibble. We miss seeing your smiling face each Sunday, and we are praying for your quick recovery.

Chapter Seventeen

Christmas

Family unity; what a magnificent and enjoyable blessing. Being encircled by sons, daughter-in-law and grandchildren is a display of beautiful word reflections and a wealth of awesome love expressions. Being surrounded by loved ones is a wonderful treat as we celebrate **Christ**mas and look forward to the beginning of a new year in the coming week. We anticipate the New Year filled with love, joy and peace abound, and remember to give thanks that His grace and mercy are the reasons we continue to linger around.

What a wonderful gift from above, the joy of having a son to treasure and shower with love. Through times of great laughter and a few tears, we lovingly journey together through the years. You bring a wealth of happiness to our lives and for that our prayers are thanks and gratitude filled. Today we celebrate **Christ**mas and the joy of Christ's birth; we are so wonderfully blessed to be united with you and loved ones on this earth.

Today, we celebrate **Christ**mas, His birth, death and resurrection; acknowledging He is King. Today, I also celebrate the joy of sharing this season with you and all the undeserved blessings it brings. Today, we celebrate with loved ones; a time of sharing, caring and a time to reflect. Because of His unnumbered mercies, we honor and praise Him with no cause to defect and through all of our weakness and imperfections, our needs He does not neglect.

Today's celebration is all about **Christ**mas, and we join in the celebration by expressions of being nice. The sharing of gifts is a wonderful thing, but we must also remember to give thanks for all kindness our loved ones and friends bring. So celebrate this holiday season by having lots of fun with family and friends, and it will seem as though your birthday celebration is starting over again. We love seeing the joy on your face as you move about opening your gifts, and the smile on your face gives our hearts a big lift.

We celebrate Black History Month and why not all the fuss as contrary to myriad beliefs, our race is definitely not a cuss.
We are gifted, unique people, proud and abundantly blessed and because of His grace, we need not worry if we surrender and all our sins confess.

Chapter Seventeen: Christmas

We acknowledge that we are His children and our countenance reveals an inner smile; providing boldness to endure difficult seasons and strength to go the extra mile.

We rejoice and celebrate our rainbow hue and resilient spirited race. We must remember our ancestors' struggles, and contributions, and pledge their sacrifices and memories forever to embrace.

We are gracious and supportive people, and proud to be in this multi-colored race; trusting and obeying Jesus, and forever dependent upon His infinite mercy and grace.

Expressions From the Heart

Chapter Eighteen

Additional Poems

Aha! You thought we had no individual pictures of you. That would have been such a shame; no way could we have allowed this to happen as how could we endure such awful pain. So scan these photos and allow your heart to swell, you were chubby, sort of handsome and strong-minded as h_ _ _. Many of your traits are so very reflective of mine that often times I quietly chuckled, but reluctantly had to decrease your playing time. Genealogy traits repeat themselves, and it is incredibly noticeable in your child; when I observe her persona, I remember you and cannot resist a smile. You were so amazing at the things that you did and said, and I often pondered what thoughts were spinning around in your head. You questioned your first name, as it was not the same as father and brother; you thought it was not fair and that your name be the same as the others. You questioned your birth date, why it came at the end of the year; what I want you to realize is that in my heart you are so exceptionally dear.

The bridge between two sisters deteriorated and fell to the ground; the pieces shattered, scattered and appeared hopeless toward any means of rebound. The bond between them was amazingly powerful, seemingly at times they were joined at the hips; now there are expressions of animosity in their attitudes and flowing from their lips. Your parents would be disillusioned and disheartened if residing upon this earth; their prayers would be for your reconciliation and reseeding of each others turf.

Hurts, not easily forgiven, but in truth we all play a significant part; however forgiveness is necessary to eradicate the unpleasantness from your hearts. The scares will not fade if you refuse to massage quietly and gently with balm; hurts require healing if you are to have peace and rest in His arms. Your adherence to this teaching will bring incredible joy, and ensures unmerited grace and alms.

Love without boundaries is undeniable and fundamental to growing closer to Christ, as without forgiveness your blessings will diminish and continually be sacrificed. Pray for guidance and allow Christ to illustrate amenable ways; He will restore your relationship healthier than in bygone days. It does not matter where the fault lies; just rebuild the bridge before either of you dies. If not, you will experience no peace when you lie down or when you rise, and unable to stop the endless tears flowing from your eyes. I love you a lot and, therefore, vested in uniting the family pot.

Chapter Eighteen: Other

What am I to do, what am I to say; why have I allowed you to continually mistreat me this way? You turned my life upside down and instead of a smile, my face is wearing a constant frown. I allowed you to break my spirit and trample my life's dreams; you were deliberately mean and deep within all I wanted was to cringe and scream.

There was a time when I had no desire to live without you; I didn't even have the strength to try, considered you my sunshine and thought only you could put a twinkle in my eye. Never again will I allow anyone to hold me captive and make me undeservingly grieve; I recognize my self-worth and know how to freely breathe. I can now boldly love myself, respect myself, give of myself and not let go. I am married to a Man who wiped my sin-plate clean; He smoothed my fears, restored my esteem, and my life He unselfishly redeemed.

Now that I've found Jesus, you no longer matter to me; you are not even a blimp on my radar and distant as the sun from the sea. Nothing is the same as now I have salvation and in the Book is written my name. How can I not praise Him now that I have been changed? My life is no longer mundane because Jesus changed me on the inside and a spirit-filled life I will maintain.

The Oakland Raiders have always been your team and we think that's terrific and super great. But when are they going step up to the plate; follow through on first downs and gain some yardage ground. They must start winning some of their games if they want to salvage their previously impressive name. The season is coming to a dismal end, and it seems that next season the Raiders will have to recruit more than a few good men. Coach must try harder to reshape his men, revise the trend, make more touch downs and score some wins. He's doing his best to be rough and tough, but just doesn't seem to have the right stuff or skillful enough; therefore, to win more games he has to use some other stuff. The Coach is trying diligently to do his best and endure the test, but unfortunately, management may release him from this mess. You are a diehard fan and we think that's great, although we are sure at times their many losses are daunting and hard to take. You have been a loyal fan for so many years, and I can understand if some of their plays cause you to almost drop a few tears. Don't despair, get discourage and root for the other team, as Raider fans are unwavering and continue to dream of recapturing the glory days of being a winning team. There is always next season

---

I awakened this morning and to my great surprise; the sun was brightly shinning and dazzled my eyes. I checked the bedside clock and it was past time to rise. I leaped out of bed, proceeded to do my usual things and wouldn't you know the phone began to ring. I became so engaged with doing this and that, I forgot to thank God and that's no insignificant fact. I bowed my head, offered up praise, and thanked Him for abundant blessings and clothes on my back as without His lovingkindness, all material possessions I would lack.

When I awakened this morning all I could say was thank you for choosing me to stand life's many tests today. I looked around, acknowledged the handiwork that displayed a minuscule of God's best, and awed that I am created as a component of the crest. Realizing my thanks is not adequate enough, my unrelenting prayer is to obey and not waver and falter under stuff. I want my life to reflect His love, mercy and glory; shining so others will know that He is the Only and is indeed worthy. When the angels awaken you each morning and you don't feel your best, sincerely give thanks for His new mercies and allow Him to do the rest.

Encouragement

Don't listen to psychic counsel or allow negative strategies to break your stride, cause your knees to buckle or bring tears to your eyes. You are fearfully and wonderfully made, the Word said it was so; just cling to biblical truth as that's the means of persevering through life's difficulties and continuing to spiritually grow. Life is an enormous challenge, oftentimes presenting concerns we least expected, but that's not cause to be discouraged or become a despondent wreck. Pick yourself up and dust yourself off; never forget that the dirt from which you were created is healthy and tough, therefore, stronger than any man-made stuff. Pray for the naysayer and continue your quest to make heaven your goal for eternal rest.

Order Page

To order additional copies of *Expressions From the Heart* please fill out the order form below and send it to us along with a check payable to:

CSN
833 Broadway, Suite 201
El Cajon, CA 92021

Or you may call our toll free order line at:
1-866-484-6184.

Expressions From the Heart

Please rush me _____ book(s) at $12.95 each.	$_____
I am enclosing $2.95 shipping and handling per book. _____ book(s) x $2.95 each =	$_____
Total enclosed:	$_____

Printed in the United States
90233LV00002B/1-99/A